FIND IT!

The Inside Story at Your Library

by Claire McInerney
illustrations by Harry Pulver

Lerner Publications Company • Minneapolis

Library of Congress Cataloging-in-Publication Data

McInerney, Claire Fleischman.
Find It! : the inside story at your library/by
Claire McInerney ; illustrations by Harry Pulver.
p.   cm. – (Study skills)
Includes index.
Summary: Describes the numerous resources, new and old, of the
library and describes how to use them.
ISBN 0-8225-2425-2 (lib. bdg.)
1. Libraries–Juvenile literature. 2. Study, Method of–Juvenile
literature. [1. Libraries. 2. Study, Method of.] I. Pulver,
Harry, ill. II. Title. III. Series: Study skills (Minneapolis, Minn.)

Z665.5.M37   1989   89-34032
025.5′6762′5–dc20   CIP
                                                          AC

Manufactured in the United States of America

1 2 3 4 5 6 7 8 9 10 99 98 97 96 95 94 93 92 91 90 89

Contents

Acknowledgements

I would like to thank Elaine Wells, who patiently provided me with a fifth-grader's view of using the library. Liz Fleischman, Cath Fleischman, and Paul Baum gave me their careful recollections of finding information when they were in elementary school.

Charon Tessman helped provide the media point of view for the book. I am also grateful to Don Roberts of Independent Media for his ideas and suggestions. Gretchen Wronka and the children's librarians in her seminar gave honest critiques. I thank them. I would also like to thank Steve Fesenmaier of the West Virginia Library Commission, whose philosophy of information and libraries has influenced my own thinking.

I would also like to acknowledge the encouragement, suggestions, and ideas of my colleague Mary Wagner.

Introduction

Step inside and look around. There's more to the library than you see at first glance. In fact, it may not even be called a library. In some schools, the library is now called the *media center* or the *resource center*.

Libraries have new names because librarians understand that, as we move into a new century, we may need new and more complex information. Computers and technology are also changing the way things work in libraries. We are now living in an information age, and those who have high-quality information have power. There are wonderful books and interesting magazines in every library, but there are also videos, audio tapes, computer games, movies, and other great things for you to use and take home.

In one way, the whole world is an information center because there are so many amazing things to learn all around us. Different kinds of rocks and fossils teach us about prehistoric times. Birds teach us about aerodynamics. The clouds teach us about the atmosphere and weather patterns.

There is one place close to your school or home, though, that has information just for you, your family, and your friends. By getting acquainted with your own library and the librarians who work there, you can:

- find the answers to everyday questions,
- get help with your homework,
- find things to do,
- solve problems, and
- get exciting books to read, newspapers, and other good information.

The librarian's job is to help you, so don't be afraid to tell her or him what you need. Ask questions too. Really, they don't mind. Remember that boys and girls have a right to information just as adults do. The library is a place where information is alive. Come on in!

A library card is the key to a world of
information and fun.

How to Talk "Library-ese"

Hola Amigos [Hello friends]

If you want to go to Mexico, it's smart to learn some Spanish. Knowing just a few Spanish words will help you order food from a menu and find your hotel. As you get better at *español*, you can meet people, make friends, and talk with them.

The library or media center is not a foreign land, but you'll feel more at home there if you know the vocabulary. Learning a little library-language will help you navigate the many paths to awesome information. Step right up and talk the librarian's language.

Learning Library Mysteries

Here are some basic code words to help you become a library insider:

Patron — In ancient times a patron was a wealthy supporter of the arts. Today a patron is a regular customer or client. This means that you are a **patron**, an important person, when you enter the library's doors.

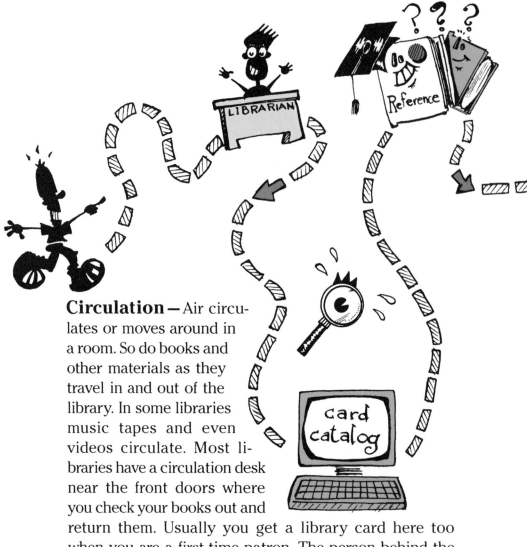

Circulation — Air circulates or moves around in a room. So do books and other materials as they travel in and out of the library. In some libraries music tapes and even videos circulate. Most libraries have a circulation desk near the front doors where you check your books out and return them. Usually you get a library card here too when you are a first-time patron. The person behind the circulation desk is either a library clerk or a library assistant.

Reference — The reference area is where special fact books are placed that can help you answer questions.

These books are used so often by so many people that they do not circulate out of the library. You can count on them always being there. At large libraries it can take a whole room to hold all the reference books. Some libraries divide up the reference books so that, for instance, books listing song titles and music awards are at a desk in the music section. If your library is arranged like this, the circulation clerk or library assistant might need to know what kind of information you need before he or she can tell you which librarian to ask. **Encyclopedias, dictionaries, atlases, almanacs,** and **indexes** are examples of reference books. They are powerful information tools.

A librarian usually works at a reference desk and directs people to the best information. Ask at the circulation desk for the reference librarian when you have a question.

Indexes — If you have used information books, you have seen an index, or list of topics, in the back of the book telling you which page has information on a certain subject. Did you know that most magazines and news-papers have indexes too? The index, usually in the form of a large book, lists the subject and then tells you exactly which issue of a magazine or newspaper has the infor-mation you need. It gives the page number too. This really beats looking through every magazine on the shelf to find a story about your favorite football team or tennis star.

The telephone yellow pages is a kind of index listing the location of services, their address, and their phone number. Large libraries collect telephone books from major cities all over the country. Before you and your parents travel, you can look up stores, restaurants, and places to visit by using the telephone book section in the library.

Fiction — Mysteries, fantasies, horror tales, stories of all kinds are called fiction, because they are not really books of facts even though they may be based on true events. **Novel** is another word for fiction or a tale that takes a whole book to tell. **Science fiction** is a kind of story that draws on what we know or might someday learn about our universe. Sometimes science fiction writers predict the future with true accuracy. Arthur C. Clarke included satellites and space stations in his science fiction books many years before any satellites were successfully launched to travel around the earth.

Nonfiction—As you can probably guess, nonfiction is true, factual information, since it is not a made-up story. Nonfiction sources will help you out when you need to understand how to do something, when you want to read about someone's life, or learn about history, animals, nature, or other parts of the world. Many athletes now watch nonfiction videos to learn how to improve their tennis serve, their golf stroke, or the way they swim.

Stacks—Fiction and nonfiction books and sometimes videos and tapes are placed in rows of shelves. The collection of shelves is referred to as the stacks.

Periodicals—Newspapers or magazines that are published at a set time (every month, every week, or every day) are called periodicals. You can find *Cycle*, *Newsweek*, *Sports Illustrated*, and *Seventeen* magazines in the periodical section of the library.

Microforms—You can imagine how much space it takes to store years and years of magazines and newspapers! They are extremely heavy and bulky. Still, researchers need old periodicals so that they can look up events in the past and find out what people of the time thought about the happenings. Librarians and media specialists have solved the storage problem by using microforms.

Microforms are tiny photographs on special kinds of film. Years of magazines and newspapers can be stored in a small space on rolls of **microfilm**, one type of microform. Or periodicals and their indexes can be photographed on sheets of film (each the size of a 3" X 5" index card) called **microfiche**. Microfiche is pronounced "my-crow-fish."

Microfiche and microfilm cannot be read with the naked eye, but libraries have machines that allow you to read an article on film and even print it out on a piece of paper. Ask the librarian or media specialist to show you how to use the microfilm reader. It's not hard once you know how.

Call Numbers — A special series of numbers (and letters) is given to each piece of material in the library. The **call numbers** are printed on each book or item to help you find what you need. In the old days, patrons would "call up" a book by writing the title and the call number on a slip of paper. Then a library employee would get the book from the stacks, which were not open to the public. This is still the way you get a book when you go to many large libraries, including the Library of Congress in Washington, D.C. Even though the Library of Congress was established for U.S. Congress members, scholars and researchers from all over the world now use the famous library. In other libraries the call number lets you find a book by yourself. The call number is like a street address for the book, telling you where to find a book on the shelves.

```
The adventures of a two-minute werewolf. DeWeese,
  Gene. Doubleday, 1983. 132p. SUMMARY:
  Fourteen-year-old Walt, discovering in himself a
  tendency to turn into a werewolf, puts his talent
  to constructive use in thwarting the activities of
  a gang of burglars. 803880411                    [B]

Adventures of a vintage car collector. Radcliff, Alan
  L. Seemann Pub.,1972. 196p. 801101320    [629.2222R]
```

This is a catalog entry as you might see it on microfiche. The call number or location of the book is the last item in each entry in this catalog, and is shown inside brackets [ ].

Classification Systems — Suppose you had to start a library with boxes of books and empty shelves. Wouldn't it make sense to put all the books about animals in one place and all those about cars together in another place? Of course, materials in a library *are* placed together with other things about the same subject.

The **Dewey decimal system** is used in most school libraries and many public libraries. The **Library of Congress system** is used in most college and university libraries, special libraries, and some public libraries.

How can you tell if your library uses the Dewey decimal system (DDS) or the Library of Congress (LC) system? It's pretty simple: Dewey call numbers begin with a number (such as 200, 300, 400), and LC call numbers begin with a letter. Here are the main categories for each system:

Subject	Dewey	LC
General Works	000	A
Philosophy	100	B
Religion	200	B
Social Sciences	300	H
Language	400	P
Pure Science	500	Q
Applied Science	600	T
Arts & Recreation	700	N
Literature	800	P
History	900	D, E, F
Biography	920	CT
Libraries	020	Z

Catalogs — Every library has a list of the things it owns along with the call numbers for each item. Patrons can check this catalog to find what the library owns about a topic and to learn the call numbers for the items they want. The catalog of items can be on cards in drawers (called the **card catalog**), in large books, on microfilm or microfiche, or on a computer.

The titles, subjects, and authors are listed alphabetically in the catalog. Just as everyone in the phone book is listed last name first, authors are listed in the library catalog that way too. Here's a record from a catalog:

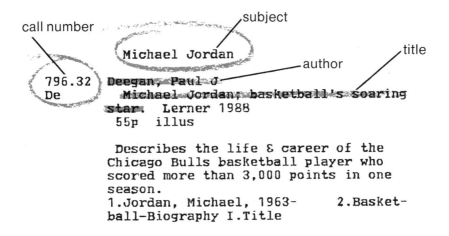

This is a "subject card," showing a book about the subject "Michael Jordan."

Chapter 1: Insider Activities

To help remember the library vocabulary in this chapter, work on these activities.

1. Draw a map of your favorite library or media center. Label the circulation desk, the reference area, the card catalog or the computer catalog, the periodicals section, and the stacks with fiction and nonfiction

materials. Fill in details of the parts of the library you like best.

2. Find three books on the library shelf that look interesting. Write down the *author's name* (the name of the person who wrote the book), the *title of the book*, and the *call number*. Does your library use the *Dewey decimal* system or the *Library of Congress* system? (Hint: most school libraries use Dewey.)

3. Interview the **librarian** or **media specialist**. If you have a tape recorder, put the interview on a cassette tape. Here are some sample questions.
   - What do you like best about your job? What do you like least about your job? What training or education did you need for your job?
   - What are some interesting questions patrons have asked you? How did you find the answers?
   - What materials do you have that are *not* books or magazines? Are these materials listed in the catalog? How are they listed?
   - Do films and videos circulate from your library? What are the circulation rules for things that are not books?

Zebra Stripes and Alphabet Bytes

Most librarians today depend on **computers** more and more to help organize, catalog, and circulate library materials. If your library is computerized, the first step in finding information will be to sit down at the computer terminal and read the instructions.

Usually you have to press certain keys on the keyboard or spell special words to ask the computer a question or give it a command. Think of the terminal as your robot, your information assistant who is going to work for you to get you what you need. You are its master, so you have to tell it what to do in a language the robot can understand.

Find lobsters is one command you might give the computer if you want to know about the lives and loves of lobsters. If the terminal comes up with a big zero, that could mean that your library has no books that are only about lobsters. What else do you know about lobsters? You could try looking under *sea animals* or *shellfish*.

Either one of these would probably get you to lobsters, but they would give you pretty big groups of entries to check for lobster information. Since lobsters are part of the animal family *crustacean*, you could also try *Find crustacean*. Bingo, the computer lists the title and call number of a book. Once you have the call number, you can look at a library map or the signs on the shelves to find your book, or ask the librarian to help you find the call number category on the shelf. Look for the book's "address" (call number) in the stacks. Then look up the part about lobsters in the book's index, and (Yay!) you'll have lobster facts.

Zebra Stripes

Congratulations. You have made your way through the catalog and have found something on the shelf. Now that you have the book in your hand, you might notice a black and white label on the book like this:

It's called a **bar code** because the stripes look like bars on a window, but it is actually a unique code for that book that can be put into a computer. Your library put the bar code on the book to make it easier to keep track of it. If the library has six hardcover copies of *Be a Dinosaur Detective*, each copy would have a different bar code. There may be another bar code on the back of the book, a code that looks like this:

This code is printed on the cover of the book by the

book's publisher. It helps the publisher (and any bookstore that happens to sell the book) keep track of books with the same title. All of the publisher's hardcover copies of *Be a Dinosaur Detective* would have the same publisher's bar code.

If your library or media center uses library bar codes on materials, then it has an **automated circulation system**. Your library may put its bar codes inside the book rather than on the back, but it serves the same purpose.

Here's how an automated circulation system works: When you check out a book, the person at the circulation desk zaps the book with a laser beam. The laser "reads" the bar code and changes that information into on-off electrical signals for the computer. The signals form words (called *bits* and *bytes* in computer language) representing the letters and numbers of the book's title, the author, and call number.

The laser will also read the bar code on your library card so that the computer knows exactly who checked out the book. The date, name of the library, and other important information is already in the computer.

In libraries that have computerized or automated circulation systems, you can even look up a book or a film in the catalog and find out from the librarian if it's checked out or on the shelf. The librarian will never tell you who has the item, though, because that is private information.

If your library or media center is not **automated** yet

by having a computer catalog and a computerized circulation system, it may be soon. Some libraries even have personal computers and computer software for your learning and fun. Media centers often have computer learning games you can play with your friends! The program *Rocky's Boots* (The Learning Company, Menlo Park, CA), for example, lets you practice solving problems. The whole point of computers in libraries is to help you find information faster and more easily.

Chapter 2: Insider Activities

1. If the grocery store where your parents shop has bar codes on items and laser readers at the checkout counter, ask the manager how they work...or ask the manager to come to your school to explain to your class how the laser beam reads the bar code into the computer. Compare the bar codes on candy bars or soup cans with the bar codes on books or tapes.

2. Compare the library's bar code with the bar code printed on the cover. Ask your librarian why the library doesn't use the bar code that the publisher has printed there.

3. Look up *Morse code* in an encyclopedia or in the card catalog. Read about how it works for sending messages. Then look up the history of computers under *computers* in the encyclopedia or in a basic

book on computers. Find out about bits, bytes, and how letters and numbers are turned into computer signals. How are a computer language and Morse code the same? (Hint: They both depend on on-off signals.) How are they different?

4. Did you know that the word *laser* is really an *acronym* (a word made up of letters from other words)? Look up *laser* in the dictionary to find out from which words the letters L A S E R are taken. (Hint: Look in one of the very large dictionaries that are usually on a special dictionary stand in the library.)

3

Finding It!

Reference Books Answer Everyday Questions

If you are curious (one sign of a smart and clever person) questions cross your mind every day. You may wonder:

- What kind of animal is a *whippet*?
- When did people first eat *pizza*?
- How many states does the *Mississippi River* flow through on its way to the Gulf of Mexico?
- How many people live in *Dallas*, Texas?
- Where can I find a poem about *fog*?

Answers to these and many other common questions can be found in reference books. They are chock-full of information. When you are at home and you phone the public librarian with a question, he or she often uses the reference books to find the answer.

Dictionaries

Your own home might have one of the most common kinds of reference books, a **dictionary**. Words are listed alphabetically in the dictionary so that you can use this book to look up the spelling or exact meaning of a word.

You may not know that many dictionaries also include a *biographical names* section that gives the correct spelling of a famous person's name, the time the person lived, and his or her main accomplishment. A **gazetteer**, giving the correct pronunciation and spelling of geographical locations, is also included with many dictionaries.

How do you look up a word in the dictionary if you don't know how to spell it in the first place? Girls and boys in school often ask this question. The answer is "Guess!" Usually you can figure out how the word begins. From there, you browse in the dictionary until you find it, just as you would browse in the record bins in a music store for a record or tape by a group you have heard on the radio but whose name you have never seen written out in print. In addition to general word dictionaries, the library has special dictionaries that define words from one subject, such as a *computer* dictionary or a *music* dictionary. There is even a dictionary of slang! The *Oxford English Dictionary* tells you the history of a word (the etymology), when it was first used, and from which country it comes.

Encyclopedias

An **encyclopedia** is a great place to start to look up an answer. An encyclopedia comes in a set of 20 to 30 books, with articles and pictures of almost all common (and some uncommon) subjects. Subjects are arranged alphabetically, but it is still a good idea to check the encyclopedia's index (if there is one) to find all the information on a certain subject. Older students often use the *Encyclopedia Britannica* or the *Encyclopedia Americana*, but most elementary school students use the *World Book Encyclopedia* or *Compton's Encyclopedia*.

Just as some dictionaries are all about one subject, an encyclopedia can be built around just one subject too— for example, *The Complete Encyclopedia of Hockey*. An important encyclopedia to help you answer science questions is the *McGraw-Hill Encyclopedia of Science and Technology*.

Who's Who

One very good place to find information about people is a who's who book. Over 200 who's who volumes have been published in the United States in the past 10 years. Who's who books give you information about important people who are living. You may want to check on these who's who reference books: *Who's Who in Rock Music, Who's Who in America, Who's Who Among Black Americans*, and *Who's Who in Karate.*

Almanacs and Atlases

Sometimes you need a fact fast, such as the name of the United States city with the most people. An **almanac** will give you an answer right away. An almanac is one book that is published every year, so the information is very current. There is a good index in each almanac so you can look up your answer quickly.

The *Information Please Almanac, Atlas and Yearbook* is a popular one that is known to have accurate statistics and lots of information about current events, countries, and sports. Check the date of the almanac to make sure that it is a recent edition.

An **atlas** is the reference book to use when you need a map. Atlases show more than the locations of cities and towns. They also illustrate rivers, mountains, and deserts in a country. Many students use the *Hammond World Atlas* because of its fine attention to detail and colorful maps.

Indexes

An **index** is an alphabetical listing of topics or names in the back of a book that tells you the page where you can find the topic or name. An index is also the name given to a book that lists a category of things and tells you where to find them.

To find a poem on a certain subject, by a favorite author, or by its title, look in *Granger's Index to Poetry*. This index will tell you the title of the book that has the poem you want in it.

Another reference book and kind of index will help would-be writers. It is the *Market Guide for Young Writers* by Kathy Henderson. If you have written your own story, play, or poem, this book will tell you where you can get it published, even though you're not yet an adult. It also gives you helpful hints on how to get your writing ready to be published. The stories of other young writers and their first publishing efforts might encourage you to keep trying.

Other indexes can help you find information about

people, record albums, and sports statistics. An example is the *Biography Index*, which tells where to find information about people in magazines and books.

By the time you finish school, you will know the reference section of the library like an old friend. You can always find answers to your question by looking up a whole book on the subject, but reference books will give you answers to most of your questions quickly.

Chapter 3: Insider Activities

1. Figure out the type of book most likely to have the answer to these questions:

- When did people first eat *pizza*?
- What does the word *whippet* mean?
- How many *states* does the *Mississippi* flow through?
- How many *people* live in *Dallas, Texas*?
- Where would you find the name of a book that has a *poem* about fog in it?

2. Pretend this is a scavenger hunt, and the answers to the questions in activity #1 are the things you must find. Track down the "treasures" in the reference section of the library. If your library is very large, look up the reference books first in the catalog to get the call numbers. A librarian can give you help if you get stuck.

3. Look up your state and home town or city in an atlas. If you or your grandparents, great-grandparents, or other relatives came from another country, find the country in the atlas.

School Reports

Get Ready for Research

Finding a fact, a fast answer, or a statistic is one thing, but when you need a lot of information, you really need to dig in and investigate. **Research** means to search thoroughly. It's a bit like being an information detective, hunting for all the clues you can find on a subject. When you're ready for research, have some sharp pencils handy and bring a packet of index cards with you for taking notes.

Periodical Indexes

Newspapers and magazines have some of the best information in the world, because journalists are pretty good information insiders themselves. Finding the information you need can be tough, though, because there are so many magazines and newspapers from which to choose. The key to finding information in periodicals (remember, that's what newspapers and magazines are called) is to look up your subject in a **periodical index**.

The index will tell you the title of the publication, the date, the name of the article, the author, and exactly which page has your subject. It may even tell you whether the article is illustrated. Of course, you have to remember to write all this down because the indexes do not circulate. Many people use the periodical indexes each day, so they cannot be checked out of the library (or circulated).

The *Reader's Guide to Periodical Literature* covers about 180 periodicals (your library may not have all of these periodicals). The index should be easy to find because the many green volumes are usually in a handy place for all to use. The *Reader's Guide* comes out twice a month, and the newer issues will be in paperback. Each issue indexes articles that appeared in a certain time period.

Here's an example of how it works: because you play the violin and the accordion, you decide to do a report for school on zydeco music, a type of folk music from the Louisiana river country that uses both instruments. You look up *zydeco music* in the *Reader's Guide* and find this listing:

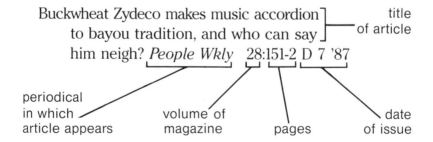

The name of the article is "Buckwheat Zydeco makes music accordion to bayou tradition, and who can say him neigh?" It sounds as if it's about a musician named Buckwheat Zydeco. It appeared in the magazine *People Weekly*, in volume 28, on pages 151 and 152. The date of that issue of the magazine is December 7, 1987. A February 1988 issue of the *Reader's Guide* contains only one article about zydeco music, so a research detective would have to consult several issues to gather enough information for a report. A dynamite researcher would also look in a music dictionary and in recent books about music, interview someone in a local music store, talk to a musician, listen to the music itself, and perhaps view a video of a zydeco performance. Your library might have the music on cassette, record, or video to help you in your search.

Research using periodical indexes is a good beginning in learning about a subject, especially if the topic is too new to have a book published about it yet. Your media center may get the shorter version of the index—the *Abridged Reader's Guide*—which covers about 60 magazines. Another popular periodical index is *The Magazine Index*, which, as you can tell from its name, covers magazines. The *New York Times*, an important United States newspaper, has its own index, and your local newspaper is probably indexed as well. You will often find *The Magazine Index* and *The New York Times Index* on microfilm.

Computer Indexes

In the last 20 years, another new electronic item has entered the library—the computer **database**. A database is an index of information. A computer database can store the author's name, the title of the article, and the magazine name, date, and page number electronically. The librarian can type in key subject words and tell the computer to list all the articles in the database on that subject. By using a computer, a telephone, and a modem (a device that lets computers talk to each other on the telephone), very large periodical indexes can be searched at lightning speed. Better yet, you can even get the results printed out so that you don't need to write down all the article titles, page numbers, and so on.

This on-line service allows your librarian to connect with a large computer somewhere else to get lists of articles, statistics, or sometimes all the words in an article itself. Computer databases are becoming a popular way to search for subjects in back issues of newspapers, too.

Because the on-line services are new and somewhat expensive, you may be charged for a computer search in a public library. If you're lucky, though, the teachers and media specialists in your school may soon be teaching you how to do this kind of research yourself. Some database services are available to people who have home computers. Certain computer subscription networks enable you to search for and find information at home using a computer, a modem, and a telephone line.

Chapter 4: Insider Activities

1. Find one of your favorite magazines in the periodical section of your library. Pick out an article that is especially interesting to you. Investigate to see if there are any other articles on the same subject in other magazines by looking up the subject in the *Reader's Guide to Periodical Literature* or *Magazine Index*. For each listing you find, write down the:
   - Title of the article
   - Name of the magazine
   - Author (if listed)
   - Date of magazine
   - Volume of magazine
   - Page numbers of the article

2. Find three listings in the *Reader's Guide to Periodical Literature* on any one of the following subjects: football, schools, environment, farms, pets, cars, surfing, inventions, rockets, fish. Photocopy the index listing or write out the important information as you did in activity 1. See if you can find one of the actual articles in your library.

3. Ask the librarian or media specialist if there are any computer databases available for research on the topics you found listed in the periodical index.

5

Reading for Fun

Finding Good Books at the Library

In her book *An American Childhood*, Annie Dillard describes how important her library was for fun and learning when she was a girl. She collected rocks and learned all about them by reading books from her library. She also taught herself to draw by checking out "how to draw" books. Most of all, though, she had adventures, was able to travel and get lost in the amazing stories and action books from the Homewood Library in Pittsburgh, Pennsylvania.

Another writer, Eudora Welty, talks about how she read library books as fast as she could. In her book *One Writer's Beginning*, she says, "Every book I seized on, from *Bunny Brown and His Sister Sue at Camp Rest-a-While* to *Twenty Thousand Leagues Under the Sea* stood for the devouring wish to read being instantly granted."

Many famous writers learned to love books through the books they checked out of public libraries. As a teenager, Richard Wright learned about life by reading books by

Sinclair Lewis and Theodore Dreiser. Wright had to get books secretly with the help of a white friend, however, because when he was young, blacks were not allowed to have library cards at his library.

Fiction and Nonfiction

As you know by now, most of the books in the library are either fiction (novels or stories) or nonfiction (facts and true information). The fiction books for fun reading and for book reports are arranged alphabetically according to the author's last name. How can you find a book you'll enjoy? Here are a few ideas for finding books you will like:

1. Look for books by the *author* of another book you enjoyed reading.
2. Ask your *friends* about their favorite books.
3. Look for books that have *won awards*—they are usually good ones. The Newbery Medal is given for the best young people's book published each year in the United States.
4. *Browse* in the fiction section. Pull out books whose titles sound interesting. Read about the book on the inside cover of a hardbound book or on the back of a paperback.
5. Tell the *librarian* the kind of book you like. Ask for his or her suggestions of others.

Nonfiction books, of course, are arranged by a different system. It is a good idea to look in the catalog to find call numbers for the type of book you need. If you enjoy browsing, you could just ask the librarian where the books on a certain subject are located. Then browse away to find something great. Here are a few suggestions to help you select quality nonfiction books:

1. Does the author give you good information in language you can understand, without "talking down" to you?
2. Is there an index in the back of the book? Does the index help you find what you need?
3. Are the illustrations clear and easy to understand?
4. Does the information seem up to date? Find the date the book was published by looking on the back of the page that lists the book's title near the beginning. The copyright date, given with the symbol for copyright, ©, is the date telling you how new or old the book is.
5. Is the author an expert in this field? If the author is not an expert, does it seem that he or she has done good research?
6. Is the writing interesting to read?

Biography is the name given to true, factual books about real people. Biographies are in the nonfiction section. In most libraries, they are placed on the shelf all together, arranged alphabetically by the last name of the person about whom the book is written. Under this system, a book about space pioneer Neil Armstrong will be on the shelf before a book about airplane pilot Amelia Earhart. In other libraries, the biographies are shelved with related nonfiction. A biography of Neil Armstrong would be with books about space. You would need to know the call number to find it.

If you cannot find the book you need, it might be checked out by someone else. You can ask the librarian to put a *hold* on the book and to call you when the person returns it. Be sure to ask whether your library charges a fee for this service.

Some books are too large to fit on the regular shelves and might be put in the **oversized** section. Many art books are oversized. An "O" for oversized will sometimes appear on the call number to show that the book is not on the regular shelf.

Interlibrary Loan

Public libraries are joined into big networks which allow the librarians to talk to each other and share library materials. One library can borrow a book, for example, from another library. The librarians say the book is then on **interlibrary loan**. School

libraries and media centers aren't always able to have interlibrary loan, but it's always a good idea to ask. The next time you need a book that isn't available in your own library, check to see if you can get it through interlibrary loan.

Chapter 5: Insider Activities

1. Think of one of your heroes or heroines. Look in the library catalog to see if there is a biography about that person. Find the biography on the shelf.

2. Before reading the biography, look up the person's name in an encyclopedia. Find the article about him

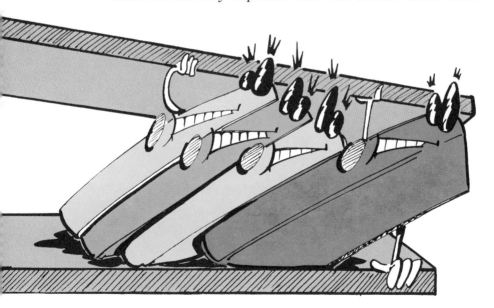

or her and read it over. The article will give you a good overall picture of the person's life.

3. Put the following last names in alphabetical order.

Anne Morrow **L**indbergh   Martin Luther **K**ing
Bob **D**ylan   Buckminster **F**uller
Pete **R**ose   Thomas **J**efferson
Wayne **G**retzky   Harriet **T**ubman
Mary Lou **R**etton   Thomas **E**dison
Isaac **A**simov   Louis **A**rmstrong

See if you can find out who these people are by using your library. (Hint: you can use the reference section and look up the names in a biographical dictionary or the encyclopedia, or you can look up books about these people in the library's biography section.)

4. What is your favorite
   • sport?
   • hobby?
   • animal?
   • food?

Using the card catalog or computer catalog, see if you can find a book, a film, or a video about your favorites. (Hint: the books will probably be on a shelf in the nonfiction section of the library stacks. The films and videos may be in a separate area.)

5. Find any of the following books in your library. They all list titles of good books and tell you what each book

is about. Find the name of a book that you think you might enjoy. See if your library has it by looking it up. If your library doesn't have the book, ask the librarian if you can get it through an interlibrary loan.

Books About Good Books

American Library Association. *Popular Reading for Children II.* Chicago: American Library Association, 1986. A collection of columns from *Booklist*, a magazine that suggests the best new books for children. Books are listed by subject, along with a description of the plot.

Association for Library Service to Children Let's Read Together Revision Committee. *Let's Read Together: Books for Family Enjoyment.* Chicago: American Library Association, 1981. Books listed are those for young people and their parents to enjoy together.

Carroll, Frances Laverne, and Mary Meacham, eds. *Exciting, Funny, Scary, Short, Different, and Sad Books Kids Like about Animals, Science, Sports, Families, Songs, and Other Things.* Chicago: American Library Association, 1984. Excellent books are listed by subject under such useful subject headings as "I Need a Book for Science Class."

Children's Book Council. *Children's Books: Awards and Prizes, Including Prizes and Awards for Young*

Adult Books. New York: Children's Book Council, 1986. This includes a list of books that have won the Newbery Medal since 1922. The Newbery Medal is awarded annually for the most distinguished contribution to literature for young people. It has been given to such books as Lois Lenske's *Strawberry Girl*, William H. Armstrong's *Sounder*, and Madeleine L'Engle's *A Wrinkle in Time*.

Friedberg, Joan Brest, June B. Mullins, Adelaide Weir Sukienik. *Accept Me As I Am: Best Books of Juvenile*

Nonfiction on Impairments and Disabilities. New York: R.R. Bowker, 1985. A detailed list of books about children with disabilities from physical problems to learning and language disabilities. Includes plot summaries.

Kobrin, Beverly. *Eyeopeners! How to Choose and Use Children's Books about Real People, Places, and Things.* New York: Penguin Books, 1988. The descriptions of books in this book by Beverly Kobrin make the reader really want to find each book and read it. This book also includes many practical suggestions for kids (for example, how to judge a book by its cover and other clues), teachers, parents, and librarians.

6

Media Makes Its Mark

By this time, you know that the library has more than books. For many years libraries have had records, tapes, and films. Some even have framed artwork you can borrow to decorate your wall. Recently, though, libraries and media centers have also collected videos, audio tapes, slides, and other interesting forms of entertainment and information. You will even find music on compact disk and computer software in many libraries.

The word **media** is really the plural form of the word *medium*, which means a way or form of sending an idea from one person to another. So paper, film, globes, maps, computer disks, even cave paintings from ancient times, are all media. Books and magazines are media too. A school library is called a "media center" because there are so many forms of information contained in this special place.

Sometimes people use the term **audio-visual materials** when referring to things in a library or media center that are not printed on paper (like books and magazines) but appeal to the ears (audio) or eyes (visual) to send a message.

In the past, many people thought that audio-visual materials or media were for fun only. It's true that a video-tape of *Back to the Future* can be lots of fun to watch, but videos can also help you with a report or research. Films, videos, and tapes can also just teach you about things in an interesting way. Here are some examples:

Owl/TV is like a science magazine on video. Taken from the Canadian television series of the same name, the programs feature topics such as how to help an injured pelican and how electric arms work. (Each Owl/TV tape is 29 minutes long. The films from 1986-88 are available in the U.S. from Bullfrog Films, Oley, PA.)

He Makes Me Feel Like Dancin' won an Academy Award in 1983 for the best documentary (true) film. It shows how dancer Jacques d'Amboise teaches children how to dance and to love dancing. (The tape is 51 minutes long and available from Direct Cinema Limited, Los Angeles, CA.)

So the next time you want to learn something new, ask your library media specialist about videos and media other than books.

Optical Disks

Everyone has heard about compact disks for music, but have you discovered **optical** or **videodiscs**? The size of a long-playing record (about 12" in diameter), these disks are shiny, silver, plasticized platters that contain much information. The information can be viewed on a television monitor in the form of moving or still pictures, written words, or sound. The soundtrack is usually narration or music. Movies were recorded on videodiscs and sold in the 1970s. Although the picture was clear and the sound was good, most people liked videotape and VCRs (videotape recorders) better. Videotape became more popular than videodiscs because people could record on tapes, but they could not record on discs.

Videodiscs are still being used for entertainment, and businesses and schools have found that they make great teaching tools. Now videodisc players are usually wired to computers so that the viewer can actively ask or answer questions. The videodisc monitor can show real moving pictures and, with a dynamic soundtrack, the learner may feel as if a teacher is sitting by his or her side. You may find some independent learning programs on videodiscs in your library or media center.

Compact Disks

Anyone who likes music knows that digitally recorded music is now available on little 4½" silver disks called compact disks or **CDs**. The compact disk uses the same technology as the videodisc; however, the CD is smaller. With disk technology advancing, more and more information can be squeezed onto this durable, easy-to-store medium. Your library media center may have music CDs.

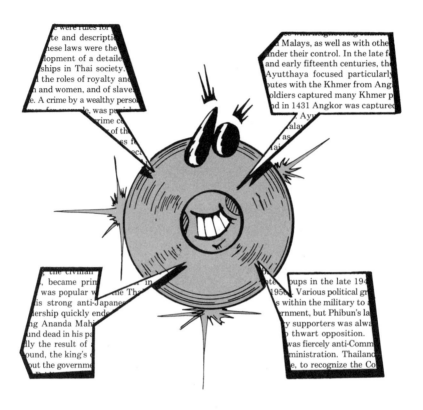

It may also have an information database on small, 4½″ optical disks, also called compact disks. You cannot usually record on these disks as you can on computer floppy disks, so they are sometimes called CD-ROMs. The ROM stands for Read Only Memory—that is, you can't write in the memory.

The same companies that produce *The Magazine Index* and the *Reader's Guide to Periodical Literature* are producing compact disks that have all the indexes from recent years on one disk. Just as the *Reader's Guide* is published throughout the year, so are information CDs. If your library has a computer and a CD-ROM reader containing one of the indexes, you can use it to find magazine articles about any subject contained in the book version of the index. Even better, you can probably get a printout of the titles of the articles too.

Forward to the Future

Some libraries now have cable television studios in their buildings, allowing people to produce their own cable television programs. In the future it is possible that the library will sponsor television meetings using satellite links to connect groups in different parts of the country or the world.

It may become routine for a student to call up the local library's electronic mailbox and type a question from his or her home computer into the library's computer. The librarian could then send the answer back by electronic mail, or he or she could call the student's home and record a message on a telephone answering device. Some libraries sponsor community electronic bulletin boards that patrons can read by using their home computers. As more school children become computer-literate, they will probably become computer library users as well.

Chapter 6: Insider Activities

1. The following popular books have all been made into

movies or videos. Find out if your library or media center has a film or video version:

Robinson Crusoe
Alice in Wonderland
Rebecca of Sunnybrook Farm
Charlie and the Chocolate Factory
The Wizard of Oz
Oliver Twist
Watership Down
David Copperfield
Moby Dick
Gulliver's Travels

2. Write a two-minute commercial for your favorite library, designed for either a radio or a television audience. Gather any players or props that you need and record the commercial on audiotape or videotape. Play the tape for your teacher or the school library media specialist.

A Library Honor Code

Students may find more reasons than ever before to use libraries in an information age. Whether the information form is electronic or paper, though, the library user must respect the materials because they belong to everyone. An honorable information user practices super manners to guarantee that he or she is always welcome in the library. Here are a few rules to follow in upholding the library honor code:

1. Take excellent care of all materials while using them. Keep them clean, dry, and safe. You are their trustworthy caretaker.
2. Return all materials on time. Someone might be waiting for one of the items you have borrowed.
3. Respect the rights of those who are using the library to study. Read quietly. Walk, don't run. Pay attention to your own work.
4. Be courteous to the librarians and other library staff.
5. Volunteer to help if equipment needs to be moved,

ABUSED BOOK CENTER

heavy boxes need to be lifted, or things need to be put away.

6. Just as if you were camping, leave the area you use in better condition than when you found it.

7. Follow rules for using the photocopier, the VCR, the computers, and other equipment. Handle them with care.

8. Share equipment and materials. If there is only one catalog, use it, and then give someone else a turn.

9. Respect the privacy of others. Give people enough room to work, and don't peer over anyone's shoulder to see what he or she is looking up in the catalog or checking out at the circulation desk. Each person's information needs are his or her own business.
10. Copy down names and titles of your sources so that you can give proper credit for ideas when you are doing a report.

Becoming a library user will allow you to be an information detective, a researcher, a reader, and maybe even a television producer or a computer user. More than finding answers to your questions, solutions to problems, and new ideas, you will find a world of fun in the library. If you actively use the library in a respectful and intelligent way, your life will become rich in information. Come in and feel at home. The library is yours to use as a tool and as a treasure. Now that you know the inside story, share it with others.

Index